CARNIVAL TIME

CARNIVAL TIME

by Vivian Sathre
illustrated by Kazu

SIMON & SCHUSTER
BOOKS FOR YOUNG READERS

Published by Simon & Schuster
New York · London · Toronto · Sydney · Tokyo · Singapore

SIMON & SCHUSTER BOOKS FOR YOUNG READERS
Simon & Schuster Building, Rockefeller Center, 1230 Avenue of the Americas
New York, New York 10020
Text copyright © 1992 by Vivian Sathre.
Illustrations copyright © 1992 by Kazu.
All rights reserved including the right of reproduction in whole or in part in any form.
SIMON & SCHUSTER BOOKS FOR YOUNG READERS
is a trademark of Simon & Schuster.
Designed by Lucille Chomowicz
The text of this book is set in Albertus Book.
The illustrations were done in pastels.
Manufactured in the United States of America   10 9 8 7 6 5 4 3 2 1
Library of Congress Cataloging-in-Publication Data.
Sathre, Vivian, Carnival time/by Vivian Sathre: illustrated by Kazu.
Summary: Describes the sights and sounds of a carnival.
[1. Carnivals—Fiction.] I. Kazu, ill. II. Title. PZ7.S24916Car
1992 [E]—dc20   ISBN 0-671-76963-4 CIP 91-44420

To Roger, Erika, Mitchell, and Karsten VS

To Meg KAZU

Music swells.
Gates open.
People enter.

Rides whirr.

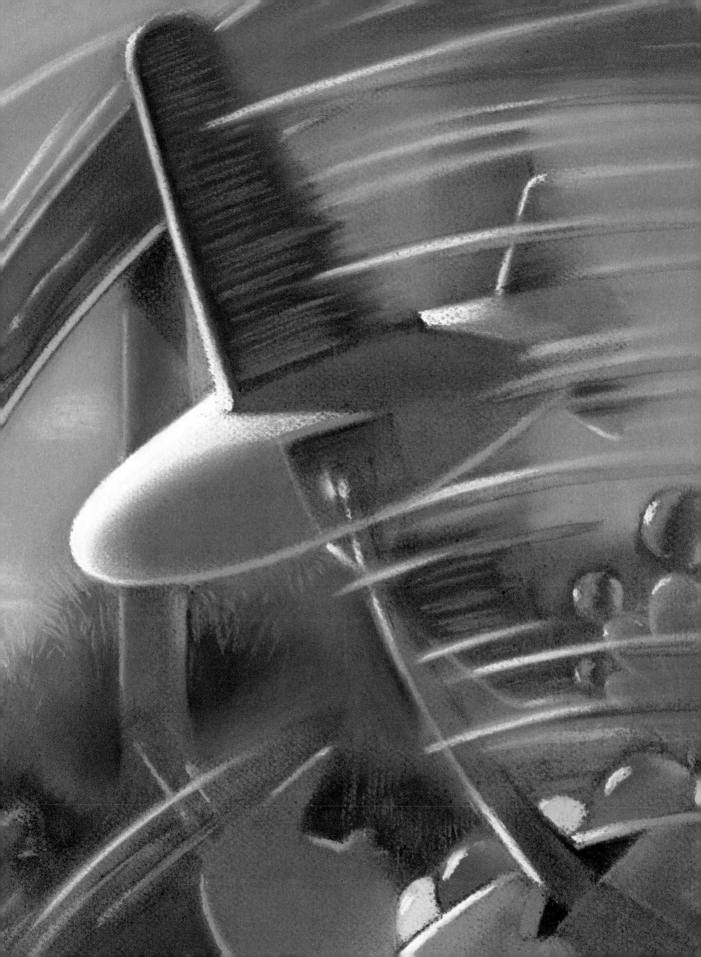

Children run.
Parents stroll.
Lines form.

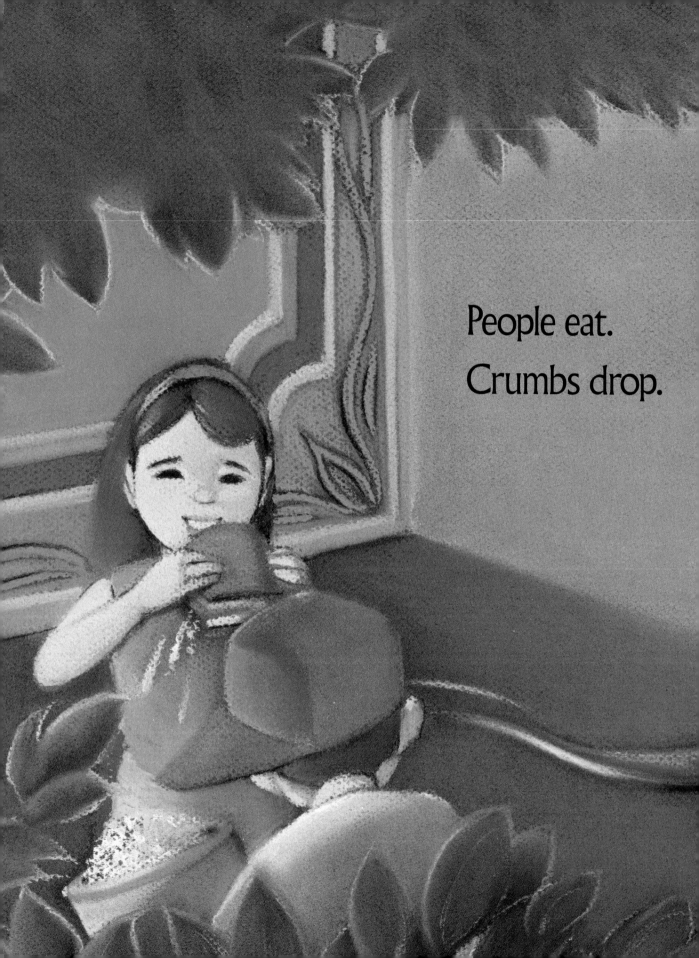

People eat.
Crumbs drop.

Birds peck.
Sweepers sweep.

Rides rumble.

Wheels spin.

Clowns clown.

Children laugh.

Balloons float.

Balloons burst.

Corn pops.

Ice cream plops.

Children cry.

Parents soothe.

Children nap.
Parents rest.

Games beckon.
Toys dangle.
Children play.

Evening comes.

Lights twinkle.